HILLTOP ELEMENTARY SCHOOL

Good Manners Matter!

Good Manners at School

Thank you!

BASEBALL

by Katie Marsico
illustrated by John Haslam
Content consultant: Robin Gaines Lanzi, PhD, MPH,
Department of Human Science, Georgetown University

magic Wagon

visit us at www.abdopublishing.com

Published by Magic Wagon, a division of the ABDO Group, 8000 West 78th Street, Edina, Minnesota, 55439. Copyright © 2009 by Abdo Consulting Group, Inc. International copyrights reserved in all countries. All rights reserved. No part of this book may be reproduced in any form without written permission from the publisher.

Looking Glass Library™ is a trademark and logo of Magic Wagon.
Printed in the United States of America, North Mankato, Minnesota.
012009
102010
Text by Katie Marsico
Illustrations by John Haslam
Edited by Amy Van Zee
Interior layout and design by Becky Daum
Cover design by Becky Daum

Library of Congress Cataloging-in-Publication Data
Marsico, Katie, 1980-
  Good manners at school / by Katie Marsico ; illustrated by John Haslam.
      p. cm. — (Good manners matter!)
  Includes bibliographical references (p.   ).
  ISBN 978-1-60270-608-8
  1. Etiquette for children and teenagers. 2. Elementary schools—Juvenile literature.
I. Haslam, John. II. Title.
  BJ1857.C5M1265 2009
  395.5'3—dc22

                          2008036320

Contents

Why Do Good Manners Matter at School?

You're sitting in math class. The teacher has just asked a question. You're excited because you know the answer. Should you raise your hand, or should you shout out the answer?

You probably spend a lot of time at school. You might already know that it's polite to raise your hand when you have something to say. Do you know why good manners matter at school?

Having good manners shows your classmates and your teacher that you care about them. Good manners will make you easy to get along with!

Think what school would be like if people didn't have good manners. No one would raise his or her hand. Students would all yell at once to answer the teacher. No one would be able to hear anyone else.

What would recess be like without good manners?
Kids would push each other on the playground.
You might not be able to use the slide or the swings.
No one would take turns.

Using good manners lets everyone have a good
time. What are some ways you use good manners
at school?

Show Good Manners at School!

There are many ways to be polite during class. Don't talk while someone else is speaking. This can be hard to do if you want to tell something to your friends. Think about when the teacher calls on you to speak, though. Do you like it if other people are talking or laughing?

When you speak in class, you want everyone to listen to what you're saying. Remember that the other kids in your class feel the same way.

Thinking of people's feelings is an important part of having good manners. Never make fun of someone who answers a question the wrong way. It's rude to laugh at a person who doesn't know the same things you do. It also hurts that person's feelings.

You might see people in school who don't look the same as you. Don't laugh or point at others. It's good manners to make everyone feel welcome!

There are lots of ways to use good manners to make new people at school feel good. You can ask a new student to sit with you at the lunch table. Introduce him or her to your friends. Offer to show the person around the school. Your good manners will help the new student feel welcome.

Having good manners means showing respect. One way to do this is to pay attention to the teacher. Follow any directions he or she gives you. For example, the teacher might ask you to speak quietly in the library. This shows respect for kids who are reading or studying.

Good manners are important anywhere you go. School is just one place you should say "please," "excuse me," "thank you," and "you are welcome."

You can also show respect to other students by taking turns and sharing. You should take turns on the slide and swings. You can practice good manners by sharing library books. You can also share toys that are used during recess.

When someone isn't sharing with you, you might feel like complaining. Expressing your feelings is okay, but do it in a way that is positive. Others will enjoy spending time with you when you don't complain.

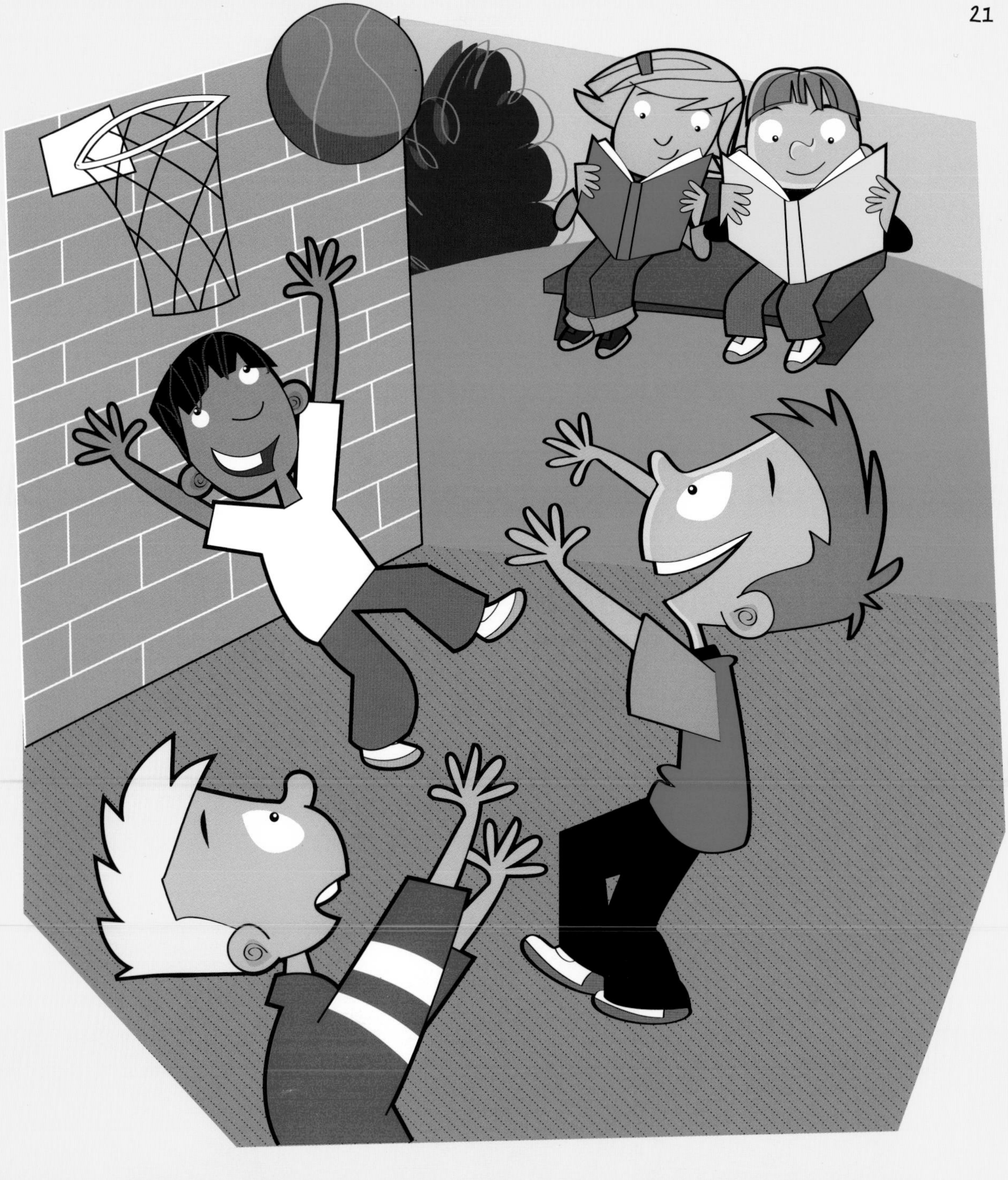

Another way to practice good manners is to help clean up. Be sure to place your trash in the garbage can. Keep your desk and locker neat.

You show respect when you do these things. You are saying that you think school is a special place and you want to take care of it. Now get ready to see some good manners in motion!

Manners in Motion

It was free reading time in the classroom. Mia was reading her favorite book about baseball. She knew a lot about sports.

A new student named Sam hoped to look at the book Mia was reading. He wanted to ask her if he could read it. Sam knew he had to ask quietly. He wanted to respect the other students who were reading.

"Excuse me, Mia," said Sam softly. "Are you almost done with that book?"

"I only have a few pages left," Mia told him. "Do you know much about baseball?"

"Not really," Sam answered. "I'm trying to learn, though."

Mia looked down at her book. "Then this book is the one for you. I've read it many times. Would you like to look at it?"

"Yes, please," said Sam. He was happy that Mia was helping him learn about sports. "Thanks, Mia!"

"You're welcome," answered Mia. "Would you like to play baseball with us at recess?"

Can you name all the different ways Mia and Sam practiced good manners at school? Having good manners is easy! Just remember to be polite. Show respect for your teachers, classmates, and school. What good manners have you practiced at school lately?

Amazing Facts about Manners at School

Taking Turns on School Teams in Japan

Kids in most schools in Japan work on teams. Teams of students take turns serving lunch to everyone in the class. Different teams also take turns keeping the classrooms and playground clean. These teams are a good example of how the students show good manners at school.

Manners at School and Schools for Manners

You know that you need to practice good manners at school. But would you have guessed that there are special schools to teach people good manners? Both kids and adults can take classes at etiquette schools. Students there learn how to be polite and respectful at work, school, and many other places.

Top Five Tips for Good Manners at School

1. Raise your hand if you know the answer to a question.
2. Don't yell or shout in the classroom.
3. Wait your turn to speak.
4. Follow the directions your teacher gives you.
5. Don't forget to say "please," "thank you," and "excuse me!"

Glossary

introduce—to present someone for the first time.
polite—showing good manners by the way you act or speak.
respect—a sign that you care about people or things and want to treat them well.
rude—showing bad manners by the way you act or speak.

Web Sites

To learn more about manners, visit ABDO Group online at **www.abdopublishing.com**. Web sites about manners are featured on our Book Links page. These links are routinely monitored and updated to provide the most current information available.

Index